The Trust Matrix

By Leon Poggioli

About the author

Leon Poggioli is a sales professional who has many years of experience selling complex solutions, mainly focused on Cybersecurity. He's worked in organisations with headcounts ranging from 20 people to over 10,000, selling to clients from startups to the ASX20.

Leon wrote The Trust Matrix after observing the way people's reputations precede them in industries where everyone knows each other.

The Trust Matrix is the definitive work on how the aggregate of human relationships in a professional community can support or hinder someone's ability to succeed, based on their reputation and how well-known they are.

He lives in Melbourne, Australia with his family.

Acknowledgements

It's extremely intimidating to take on a project like writing a book and push it out into the world to be judged by the greater community, particularly those who you deal with on a day-to-day basis.

My first thanks go to those who were kind enough to review my earlier edits and provide concrete feedback, both on what worked and on what needed improvement. Two friends who really delivered here were Peter Fraser and Charlie Forrest, both of whom happen to be great operators in their respective fields. I can tell you that this is no coincidence.

My immediate family are also owed thanks for giving me the perspective to realise that there's more to life than your day job, which prompted me to put the concept of the Trust Matrix out into the world and win a few minds to my ideas.

Finally, to the people I've interacted with over the years, you've all contributed to my experiences which have culminated into this book, and while I'm sure I haven't dealt with every single person as ideally as I outline here, I hope the net total is in the positive.

For Luca

Introduction

The Trust Matrix: The way in which a network of interconnected individuals ranks each other for integrity and dependability.

What is the Trust Matrix?

The Trust Matrix is a term I invented to describe a phenomenon I have observed in social networks - how a person's reputation stands on the opinion of the many people with whom they interconnect.

These interconnections form a matrix of relationships that each rank a person for integrity and dependability - in effect, how much you trust them. Hence, the Trust Matrix.

Think about the kind of reputation you have with every person you know. Now, lay those reputations onto a mesh of every other relationship each person has, and you get the Trust Matrix. But it doesn't stop there.

Our reputations will naturally cascade beyond the people we already know, to people we are yet to meet, by natural word of mouth.

This book is not about how to become a trustworthy and reliable person.

It's about how you can market your integrity and dependability to the industry in which you work.

What problem does the Trust Matrix solve?

Doing business with people you don't know and don't trust is very costly. You need to do your due diligence on them, and you need to make sure that any agreements you strike don't have loopholes which can be exploited. You also need to put measures in place to ensure they will hold up their end of the bargain. These things all create a huge amount of friction, making it impossible to get anything done without incurring huge cost.

I'm not just referring to business in the traditional sense of the word. Life works better when we trust our families, our neighbours, and the other people around us.

Even if you were to put every possible measure in place to protect yourself, a smart crook can always use their experience to find a way to rip you off. Without the Trust Matrix, we'd all be hermits, trying to live in total self-sufficiency because we wouldn't know whether our neighbours were like-minded folks willing to help, or crooks trying to take advantage of us.

Conducting yourself with integrity and dependability isn't an end to itself - the real reason people with those attributes succeed is that they are better positioned to create value for themselves and others.

If there's one thing you can refer back to in your conduct, it would be "Does what I'm doing create value for all the parties I'm working with?" If it doesn't, the relationship isn't serving a purpose.

People will naturally gravitate out those who are dependable and trustworthy.

Why?

Because dependable and trustworthy people deliver to expectations. Life's too short to burn time and energy dealing with people you can't trust or depend on.

The Trust Matrix is a natural human response to living in a community, where we can put an informal scorecard in place that keeps track of how a person conducts themselves over time with the people around them. Crooks are quickly found out and kicked out of the system. Dependable people with integrity compound their reputations over a lifetime to the point where they can access opportunities which trustworthy people with shorter track records cannot.

Benefits of the Trust Matrix

What's the main benefit that is achieved when everyone trusts one another?

Things happen more quickly.

Things happen more easily.

Why? Because you can do away with the due diligence and secrecy which are needed when the group doesn't know or trust each other.

People who are positioned well in the Trust Matrix will reap the rewards of greater opportunities which they can seize with less effort. Your daily interactions with others are like tiny deposits or withdrawals into a bank account - a dollar here, fifty cents there. If that doesn't sound like much, you don't understand compound interest.

For example:

- $10 a day is a $3650 annual investment.
- Over 20 years, that's about $73,000.
- Compound that daily at a 10% annual rate, and over a 20-year period your $73,000 investment has grown to $233,126.
- If you contribute nothing further and leave it to keep compounding for another 20 years, your original $73,000 investment will have grown to more than $1.7 Million, and your $10 daily outlay 40 years ago will be paying you back $465.75 per day, forever.

Over a 40-year career, compounding matters.

Warren Buffett is a great example, having started his original investment partnership in 1956. More than 60 years on, Berkshire Hathaway is one of the world's most important insurers, an industry which literally depends on the trust of your customers.

When a company founder who has spent a lifetime building their business decides they want to sell to someone they can trust to look after the business, they don't call private equity firms. They call Warren Buffett.

Warren Buffett's Vice-Chairman Charlie Munger once said:

"The highest reach of civilization is a seamless system of trust among all parties concerned"

If everybody aspired to live these words, the world would be a vastly different place.

When it comes to relationships, if you're always adding to the positive side of the ledger, it will compound to enormous opportunities over your career. If your conduct is consistently on the negative side, you'll soon be in so much "debt" that you'll never be able to recover your reputation.

The process of building a great reputation is not complicated:

1. Be a trustworthy and reliable person
2. Meet lots of people

3. Build a trusted relationship with them
4. Consistently interact with your network in a trustworthy manner.

Do these things every day, and you'll build a great reputation with a larger and larger group of people, which in the aggregate, defines your reputation in the Trust Matrix.

Once your reputation reaches critical mass, word will spread outside of your control, which is why your reputation needs to be rock-solid. If your reputation sucks, people who you've never met aren't even going to give you a chance, because they've already heard everything they need to know.

Good or bad, your reputation will precede you.

My experience with the Trust Matrix

I've observed the Trust Matrix at work in my industry -
the Cybersecurity industry in Melbourne, Australia. As a
sales professional you deal with all sorts - customers,
partners, co-workers, distributors, other vendors, the list
goes on. How these people interact with one another,
and the reputations they each have for trustworthiness
and reliability, affects the way I interact with that person.

There are people who I know I can trust to work with,
and others I'll only deal with through gritted teeth when
there is no other option.

I've also become conscious of my own reputation, and
how others in the Trust Matrix see me - because it's no
longer about 1:1 relationships - people gossip about
each other, and the stories get around. The easiest way
to maintain a good reputation is to conduct yourself with
integrity wherever you go.

What you'll learn

The purpose of this book is to open your eyes to the Trust Matrix and show you how to use it to your advantage. You'll learn how to build a bigger network, and how to build a reputation that travels well to people that you haven't yet met.

You'll learn how to compound your existing reputation and network into bigger and better opportunities, and there are also suggestions on how to handle areas of the matrix which include unreliable and low-integrity people (Henceforth referred to using Australia corporate terminology: Dickheads.)

This guide is a compilation of my own knowledge and observations. No matter what culture or industry you operate in, the Trust Matrix exists. By reading this book and incorporating its lessons into the way you conduct yourself, you'll be better equipped to interact with the people out there who are both talking to you and talking about you.

All scenarios, people and companies are totally fictional and do not represent actual people or situations. They are merely used to illustrate the kinds of situations which play out in the professional world every day.

Rules of the Trust Matrix

1. Things get done quicker and easier when all parties know and trust each other.

2. Act consistently.

3. Conduct yourself with genuine integrity.

4. Treat others how you would want to be treated.

5. Don't compromise your integrity to try and please everybody.

6. Like it or not, people will talk about you behind your back.

7. The more people you know, the better it is to have a good reputation, and the worse it is to have a bad one.

8. Actions speak louder than words.

9. Every interaction with someone is the equivalent of a deposit (or withdrawal) into a metaphorical bank account whose value equals your reputation in the Trust Matrix.

10. Your reputation will compound over your lifetime.

11. Quid pro quo - give freely before you ever decide to ask someone for a favour.

12. First impressions matter.

13. Build deeper relationships with the people who matter to you.

14. The Trust Matrix is an infinite game that people are playing, whether they like it or not, for their entire lives.

Bonus Rule: Don't be a dickhead.

Chapter 1. Don't be a Dickhead

The whole of the Bible can be boiled down to a single golden rule:

"Do unto others, as you would have them do unto you".

A similar rule is ever-present in Australian business culture:

"Don't be a dickhead."

It's been my observation that this is the most fundamental value which dictates appropriate behaviour in Australian corporate culture. The exact terminology may vary in other countries; nonetheless, it's a key guideline in deciding how you want to conduct yourself. Translation for the Americans: don't be a jerk.

What constitutes a dickhead?

Dickheads do self-serving things that nobody likes, like backstabbing, creating drama, and throwing people under the bus to cover for their own shortcomings. Dickheads often exhibit obvious deficiencies in their integrity.

A dickhead can be a man or a woman, the term is gender-neutral,

A lot of the time it's ok to be a mediocre performer, as long as you're not a dickhead. There are plenty of roles for non-star performers, but what teams won't have any room for, is dickheads.

Dickheads ruin everything by killing the energy in the workplace with their toxic vibes. If a dickhead is accidentally hired, you'd better make sure you get rid of them during their probation period, otherwise, you'll have a hell of a time fixing your mistake.

It is for this reason that many companies (or individual teams, with sensible managers) have an unwritten "no dickheads" rule.

The final stage interview with a senior manager is sometimes referred to as the "dickhead check" to make sure the candidate isn't a dickhead.

You can get away with a lot in the Trust Matrix, as long as you're not a dickhead. You can be flaky, you can sometimes not be on time. But if you're branded a dickhead by the people who know you well, you will carry the title of "dickhead" wherever you go.

Here's a real-life example: The character of Moe Szyslak in *The Simpsons* has been voiced by Hank Azaria since the first episode - but he wasn't originally cast for Moe. Moe was going to be voiced by an actor called Christopher Collins. Collins' work was great, but the other staff and actors found him so unpleasant to work with that he was booted off the show and missed out on the opportunity to play the voice of an iconic character in the greatest animated television show of all time.

So remember, don't be a dickhead.

Chapter 2. What is the Trust Matrix?

Human beings organise ourselves into groups, because we need to depend on each other to get things done. As John Donne said, no man is an island.

The way we interact 1:1 is pretty simple, but as a network of interconnected people grows, these interactions become more and more complex.

If you consider all the people you know, the map of those relationships would look like a hub and spoke, with you at the centre:

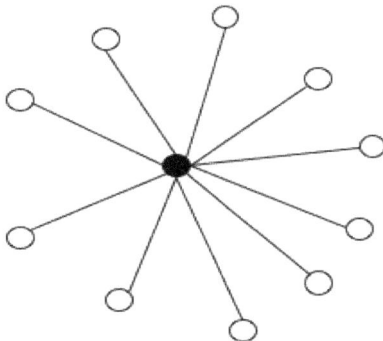

While this is how someone sees their own network, the actual mesh of relationships is much more complex.

Many of the people we know also have relationships with each other. And beyond this first degree of separation are other people you might interact with in future, who will decide how trustworthy you are based on what they've already heard about you, and the people you both know in common.

It turns out that a map of these relationships looks a lot more like this:

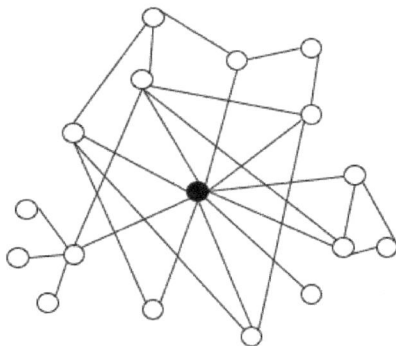

Multiply this out by the 1000+ connections many people have on LinkedIn, and you'll see how complex the Trust Matrix is. It might seem overwhelming to keep track of the broad network of relationships that mesh around you, but you don't need to understand the component parts - that's only for sociopaths who manipulate others for their own personal advantage.

By conducting yourself with integrity, a good reputation takes care of itself.

Why the Trust Matrix exists

Without the Trust Matrix, we would need to vet every new person individually and monitor how well they perform against our expectations over time. This creates unnecessary overhead to getting things done - wouldn't it be easier to just check whose word is good and who can't be trusted?

The Trust Matrix is an essential way for people to determine who they can and cannot depend on. It's an effective way to vet people you haven't yet met and an equally effective way to freeze out the people who nobody wants to deal with - something that happens naturally in workplaces the world over.

Although it primarily concerns itself with work situations, the Trust Matrix can be applied to any community of people where nobody knows everyone but is connected by 2, 3 or 4 degrees of separation through something you all have in common.

You're already aware of the Trust Matrix

Even if you've never heard of it, you already use the Trust Matrix in your everyday life. Most job offers are contingent on reference checks, and your high school football coach probably isn't going to be suitable when you're 15 years into your career and trying to land your first Junior VP role.

What are the attributes of a good reference in the high-stakes game of hiring someone for a senior position?

That would be someone who:

1. Has worked with you recently
2. Rates you highly

3. Also has a good reputation
4. Knows the hiring manager or someone senior in the organisation

It also works in reverse. Once your reputation is in the toilet with enough people, you will get secretly blackballed at every turn. You might not know who it was, but the people on the inside will do their best to keep you out if you're a dickhead. Hiring decisions are supposed to be confidential, but people are always going to ask around.

Here's a hypothetical scenario:

Jack is an experienced sales executive moving from Dallas to the San Francisco Bay Area to be closer to the tech scene. He spent 20 years at a large technology firm, took a 3 month career break and decided he wanted a new challenge. He sails through the interviews, and talks up how much experience he has selling into top companies based in Dallas, and how many executive relationships he has.

The Sales VP Monica sees Jack is connected with a couple of her old Dallas-based clients on LinkedIn, and she knows one in particular quite well after he bought from her previous company in a $2m deal which took 12 months to close. Monica drops him a message asking about Jack. The client rings her cell 2 minutes later.

"Are thinking about hiring Jack? He's an absolute train wreck. We did a lot of business with him a few years ago but he started getting too aggressive pushing products that were clearly not a fit for us and he has a problem with alcohol. We've banned him from visiting our company's offices. Nobody in Dallas will hire him and he can't afford to retire, that's why he moved out to California".

Monica wisely decided not to hire Jack.

If you find yourself in a situation like the one Jack is in, not only will you probably not know why you weren't hired, it'll be a long hard road to rebuild your reputation.

Chapter 3. You can't fake it forever

Some people say you should "fake it 'til you make it". This advice does not apply when it comes to integrity, trust, and dependability. If you're faking it, you'll either slip up at some point or people will be able to tell you're covering up your dickhead attributes with a thin veneer of BS.

There's nothing to fake when you're an honest and dependable person, and you don't need any special skills to conduct yourself that way. Trying to fake integrity while cutting corners to get ahead is a recipe for disaster.

All you need to do is conduct yourself with integrity and spread the word by getting to know as many people as possible. It's simple but there aren't any shortcuts. This means you need to be humble, hardworking, and only commit to something when you know you're going to be able to deliver.

The people who benefit from the Trust Matrix the most are fundamentally good and reliable people who conduct themselves with integrity. This makes sense because the Trust Matrix is a way for people to check whether or not they can trust somebody before they really get to know them.

It also works against people who focus on short term benefits at the expense of another person's trust. When it comes to trust and integrity, playing the long game pays off big time - just not immediately.

If you're a dickhead, you might be able to fake being a good person in the short term with a few people, but in the long run, you will get caught out, and once that happens, your reputation is hurt forever.

Example:
Sarah is an independent PR professional with a carefully curated social media profile who works hard to be photographed at the right events. She knows lots of people and always makes a great first impression. She's very charming.

Plenty of people who meet Sarah once or twice walk away with a great opinion of her, and this often leads to business. Unfortunately, most of her clients choose not to keep her on retainer for longer than 12 months. In spite of Sarah's obvious PR skills, she is quite unreliable and has been caught stretching the truth numerous times when name-dropping other clients.

Sarah works in a big city where there is plenty of business to keep her going for the next 20 years, but the amount of churn she experiences means she needs to constantly focus on maintaining her image instead of her clients.

The challenge Sarah has is that she can't scale her business, because her clients leave at the same rate at which she brings new ones onboard. Her lack of follow-through means that she's constantly hustling for new clients to pay her for a year or two before they drop her and she has to go back to the drawing board.

Doing the right thing might not always be easy in the short term, but it builds a solid foundation for the future that acts like bedrock to your reputation and career.

The people who take a "smash and grab" approach to life will hit their peak early, then enter a decline phase until they are stuck in tougher jobs (where, ironically, a good reputation would be very helpful) or wash out of whichever industry they work in.

Getting the basics right

There are seven basic standards to how you conduct yourself that I consider to be "table stakes" for anyone who takes their reputation seriously. These minimum standards are compulsory. Nothing else you do matters if you don't get these things right:

1. Show up early.

Unforeseen circumstances happen - don't let them turn into excuses (which nobody believes anyway). Showing up early also lets you get yourself into the zone, and make small talk (and a great first impression) with the people you meet beforehand, like the receptionist.

2. Pay attention.

If you play on your phone when you're speaking with someone, what message does that send about how you value their time? You've got two ears and one mouth, so let people talk and follow up their answers with more questions. Make eye contact, remember their names, and always ask high-quality questions.

3. Be Prepared.

Do your research. Have everything ready to go when you're presenting. Make sure the demo works. Don't forget your laptop charger, etc. Remember the 5 P's: Prior Planning Prevents Poor Performance. Deciding to "Just wing it" is a recipe for disaster.

4. Deliver to your commitments.

If something is held up, let people know in advance. Call people back if you say you will. Don't purposely mislead people who are relying on you. Soon they'll realise they can't rely on you and decide it's easier not to deal with you at all.

5. Don't make excuses.

Everyone's allowed a mulligan from time to time, but do it too often and nobody will accept an excuse from you ever again.

6. Maintain your integrity.

This means no kickbacks, no cheating people, no cheating your own company. As soon as people see you compromising your own integrity, you're on a slippery slope to a bad reputation.

7. Don't share secrets.

Share something you shouldn't and both parties will know they can't trust you with anything. Once word gets out that you can't be trusted with a secret, you'll be out of the loop and won't know what's going on.

The long game

There is no point in the journey of life where you sit back and go "I've made my money. I've got the corner office and the VP title. Now I can finally relax and start acting like a dickhead to the people around me".

There is no "end of the game" as far as managing your reputation - you're playing it until the day you die. Naval Ravikant's famous twitter storm on May 31, 2018 highlighted this:

"Play iterated games. All the returns in life, whether in wealth, relationships, or knowledge, come from compound interest."

The Trust Matrix operates like an infinite game. Even if you're saying goodbye to someone forever, your reputation carries on regardless.

When you're young and on the way up, some more experienced people will choose to help and guide you, and some others will either ignore you, or worse, take advantage of you. A karmic bitch-slap awaits those who look down on the young graduate who ends up interviewing them for a job 10 years later.

The Trust Matrix rewards the people who conduct themselves with integrity even after they have "made it". You'll have the opportunity to mentor others, which is immensely satisfying to do with the right people, and who knows what opportunities your reputation will set you up for even as you transition to retirement?

Every now and then, your integrity will be wrongly called into question. The best defence is a rock-solid reputation backed up by plenty of people who know you well. If you play too close to the edge too often, people won't believe you if you ever find yourself in a situation where you could really use the benefit of the doubt.

Chapter 4. It all adds up

Every interaction with every person you meet adds up to your overall reputation across the Trust Matrix. If you're doing it properly, your reputation should be consistent with people who have known you for a while. That means you're being your genuine self with people no matter who they are and what they do.

Confidence level

Your reputation isn't the only consideration. How well do people know you? Someone who has just met you is going to be less confident of their opinion than someone who has dealt with you continually for a decade.

So while a person's opinion of you can be good or bad, it can change over time, from when they first hear about you, continuing forever as they get to know you better and better. Here's a chart outlining 4 possible scenarios:

Good reputation

Good first impression		Golden Reputation

First meeting ——————————————————————→ Known each other for years

Bad first impression		Dickhead

Bad reputation

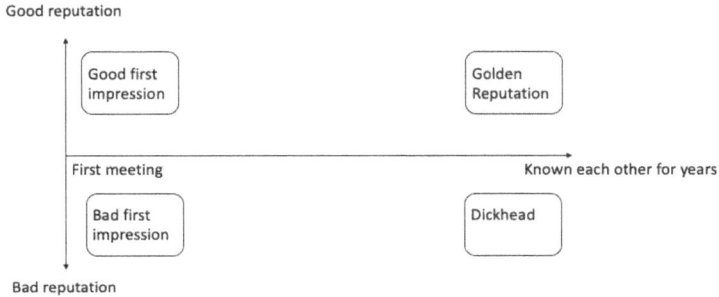

The Y-axis (up and down) represents how people rate you - the midpoint is totally neutral. The more or less someone likes you, the higher or lower you sit on that line:

Good reputation

Bad reputation

41

The X-axis (left to right) represents how well that person knows you. An initial good impression is helpful to the future of your relationship but it won't matter if, over time, they discover that you're actually a dickhead.

First meeting ————————————————————▶ Known each other for years

Early in the relationship, your reputation can change easily, because there isn't a huge track record for someone to anchor their opinion against.

Over time, their opinion of you will become firmer and firmer. This is why first impressions, while important, are only the beginning, and why it's so difficult to recover a relationship with someone who knows you well and strongly dislikes you.

You sit somewhere on this chart with every single person you know. Add them all together, and you have your position in the Trust Matrix.

How relationships evolve over time

Let's imagine some scenarios. Start with the ideal - you make a good initial impression, which only gets better over time:

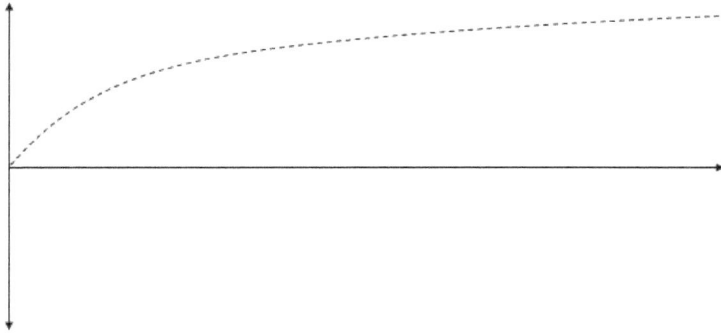

Now, a bad initial impression that you manage to recover:

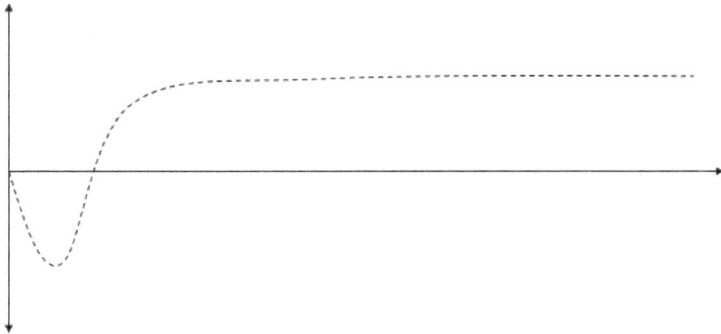

And finally, a good initial impression that you quickly destroy, with no chance of recovery, because that person wants nothing to do with you ever again:

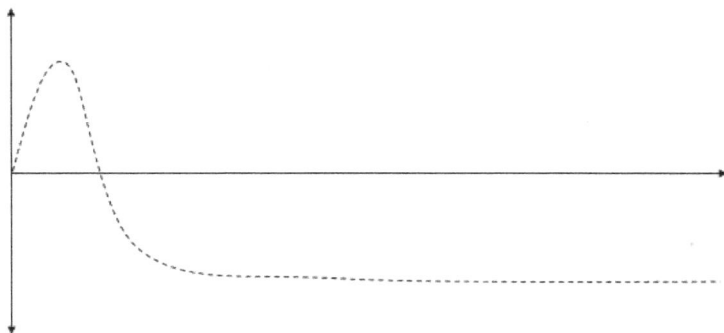

I reiterate my earlier point about first impressions: it is absolutely critical to do the right thing when you first meet someone. Most people will give someone they already know well a second chance, but do the wrong thing early on and you've burnt that relationship forever.

Sometimes you won't even get a chance to make a first impression, say if you're representing a company with a client who has been treated poorly in the past. You can't change the past, but you can control how you conduct yourself, and their opinion of you should shine through brighter than the company you work for.

The composition of your network

The value of your network isn't just about the number of people you know, it's about who they are and who else they know. Are they all co-workers who already know each other? Does your network straddle multiple groups, say across 2 or more industries? How senior are the people you genuinely know? Do you know the heavyweights of your industry or just the serial networkers who don't achieve much in the way of results?

It's important to understand the strength of your network - not to serve your ego, but because highly trusted people achieve better results with less effort - it's easier and quicker to get things done when all parties trust one another.

Building your network to create value

When people don't grow their networks effectively, they limit the opportunities available to them.

A network's value depends on its size, quality of connections and the unique value you can offer.

What is unique value? Unique value is something that sets you apart from the other people in your network. For example, it could be the ability to act as a bridge between two (or more) clusters of people who aren't otherwise connected, or a special skill that is in high demand in your network.

The below examples will limit your ability to offer unique value to your network:

Knowing a group that already knows each other (for example, all your co-workers):

Part of the value you offer with your network is the number of people you know that aren't already connected to each other. If everyone knows each other already, you can't add value by making introductions. It is, however, good to know many people in a cluster that all know each other because you can become the go-to person to make introductions to another cluster of people - you are a "bridge".

For example, if you are a lawyer whose network also includes tech entrepreneurs, you'll have a more valuable network than one consisting solely of lawyers.

The lawyers all know each other, so you're not bringing any unique value from knowing the same group of people. Where unique value comes, is in being able to connect your lawyer friends with tech entrepreneurs.

Even if your network is restricted to a single cluster of people, it is always good if that group rate you highly and will say good things about you behind your back.

Not knowing enough people:

This is worse than knowing a lot of people in the same industry, because if you know 1000 people who all work at the same company, they will start moving around through natural job attrition and your network spread will increase.

If you know very few people, you will be an almost total non-entity in the Trust Matrix. It's a hard road to travel alone, and you'll find you're constantly losing out to competitors on the basis of who they know, whether it is for jobs, sales, or other opportunities. Being a "known quantity" is a big leg up on the competition, even if you're not all that great.

Having a reputation as a "connect-a-holic": These people often brag about being LIONs (LinkedIn Open Networkers) and seem to have let LinkedIn consume any time they might have used to be effective in their jobs. Plenty of people just accept every connection, which is a great way for scammers to use 100 common connections to start connecting with people who would ordinarily be more discerning.

The real problem with being a loose networker is that you will invariably focus on quantity over quality when it comes to relationships with people in your network.

How well do you know these people? What percentage have you actually met? Who have you actually conducted business with? Who knows you well enough to put their name to your reputation in a reference check scenario?

Example: Not maintaining your network

Robert was a very experienced and capable Operations Manager in the manufacturing industry who had been with the same firm for 20 years. He started there after completing an apprenticeship as a fitter and turner, and had worked his way up without so much as an interview. He knew everybody from top to bottom, and was known as the guy who "knew how everything worked".

Robert enjoyed his work and spent most of his free time socialising with his co-workers. He didn't like travelling to company conferences or meeting with vendors, his preference was to focus on meeting and exceeding manufacturing KPIs.

Robert's company was acquired by a German firm who re-tooled the plant to manufacture parts for some of the other companies they owned. The firm also implemented new procedures consistent with their internal culture.

When the new procedures were announced, Robert pushed back hard to his new management and refused to co-operate. In a heated argument with some of the German managers, he resigned in a way that would have made it impossible for him to return to that company.

After the dust had settled, Robert realised he had no professional network and no skills when it came to searching for jobs, as he'd last applied for a job 20 years earlier. Not being currently employed, and having resigned from a company with a strong international reputation did not reflect well in the interview process.

After 6 months of searching, Robert lowered his standards to a shift supervisor role for less money and less interesting work.

Robert wasn't a dickhead. He was a reliable person who had integrity. But nobody cares about your reputation if they don't know who you are - and that was his mistake. The Robert product was excellent - but nobody knew about it. If I was Robert's mentor, I'd encourage him to do the following to work his way back up to an Operations Manager role again:

1. Remain humble and listen to others - if he'd simply gone with the flow of the new leadership, I'm sure Robert would have learned a few things from his new bosses, and would have earned their respect enough to be able to teach them a few things as well.

2. Keep in touch with industry peers by going to conferences and networking. Not only will you make new contacts but you'll learn things from your industry peers that you can apply in your own business.

3. Meet with vendors, and let them buy you lunch and coffee. Some people don't see value in meeting with sales people, but sales people are exactly the ones who know people at all the

other companies you could end up working for. If they think you'll buy from them if you go work somewhere else, they'll be happy to help you get in touch with the right people and they'll vouch for your reputation.

Chapter 5. Enriching your network

Now that you know about the mistakes to avoid, it's time to learn how to improve the competitive advantage of your reputation. Your position in the Trust Matrix is your own personal moat, in the way Warren Buffett defines a moat as a company's durable competitive advantage:

An economic moat is a durable competitive advantage one organisation has over its competitors, much as if the organisation was a castle. The deeper and wider the moat, the more difficult it is for competitors to attack it. Warren Buffett encourages the CEOs of Berkshire Hathaway companies to focus on widening their moats every year, to further protect that company's competitive advantage.

Companies with wide moats are more profitable than companies without moats, and they are likely to survive for longer because it's harder for competitors to take their market share.

If your position in the Trust Matrix is like a company, the strategy to widen your moat is to go deeper and wider in your relationships. Going deeper means getting to better know the key people in your network, and going wider means broadening your network into different clusters of people.

Superficial relationships with people are of such little value that they are essentially worthless. Relationships don't just sit on the shelf to be picked up when someone can help you - they are living things that need to be continuously fed and watered; otherwise, they wither and die.

Making deposits

The investments you make into the relationships in your professional network is much like the deposits you make into a bank account. Enough small good things over time with enough people will compound into something self-sustaining, to the point that you are turning away opportunities so you can focus on the ones which will create the most value.

On the other hand, if you make enough small "overdrafts" with enough people, those things will compound into a negative reputation that will follow you around like a bad smell. I'm referring to things like deliberately misleading someone or not following through on a commitment.

These things also serve to affect your outlook and mood. We've all had days when nothing goes right and we feel like the world is out to get us. If you have a bad reputation, you'll be having those days all the time. It's like an invisible force that's conspiring against you, and while it's not directed by a single individual, you're experiencing the Trust Matrix at work.

Most people won't go out of your way to undermine you, but you never know who is going to meet whom when they ask "hey, I'm about a make a hiring decision, can I run a couple of names past you?"

Make enough overdrafts on your reputation and you might as well pack up and find a new career.

The deposits you make on the positive side are almost a mirror image. People will go in to bat for you, defend you, and put you forward for opportunities where they have no vested interest, just because they want to help you and know you are reliable.

If your integrity is ever questioned (Guaranteed, at one point or another, someone will be convinced that you screwed them over) you'll be robust to any significant reputational damage, because whenever your name comes up, people will rush to defend you.

It's not one single action that gets you where you are in the Trust Matrix, but the sum of what you do, every day, over time.

Your balance in the Trust Matrix bank account is always going up or down, and if you do nothing, inflation will wear it down to zero. It's important to keep adding value every day by being reliable and conducting yourself with integrity.

Going wider: New clusters

New clusters refer to groups of people that sit outside your main industry network, allowing you to act as a bridge or domain expert into that cluster. For example, if you're in the tech industry, and happen to go to a manufacturing conference because lots of your customers are manufacturers, you can make a lot of new connections with manufacturing people and be seen as the go-to person to connect people from the tech and manufacturing industries together. This is much more valuable than simply being well-connected in a single industry, because fewer people can offer this, and it has the ability to create significant value with little effort.

Connecting with new clusters of people generally means moving outside of the circles you normally move in. This has the potential to significantly improve the value of your network. Why? You're not only a bridge between two clusters, you will also be seen as an authority to people outside your core domain of expertise.

Amongst plumbers, it's hard to stand out. But be known as a great plumber amongst the legal community, and you'll be able to send your kids to college off the back of lawyers' bathroom renovations.

Building on existing relationships

It's easy enough to meet someone, learn a little bit about them, connect on LinkedIn, and maintain a superficial relationship. Yes, 95% of your relationships will be like this (it's just impossible to have a big network and know every single person really well), but it's important to also make deeper relationships because these are the people who can help you achieve next-level things like access to sales opportunities and job recommendations. It goes without saying, you'll also be doing the same for them - life is a two-way street.

Hallmarks of a deeper relationship:

1. Do they call you if they're considering an opportunity to move to another firm?
2. Have you been to each other's homes and met each other's families?
3. Will they meet up with you for a coffee no questions asked?
4. Are they willing to make the effort to strongly recommend you to somebody (not just assist with a basic introduction)
5. Do you *trust* each other, beyond the level to which it's convenient to do so?

While knowing lots of people is helpful, knowing a few people really well who will move mountains for you really shows your worth as an individual and validates that you're doing the right thing.

The people you have deep relationships should also be people with a strong reputation within your Trust Matrix. They need to be people you respect and admire, and you should have this kind of relationship with multiple people in each cluster that you are connected to.

Maintaining "Dormant" relationships

Some strong business relationships end up going dormant due to circumstances. It could be a move to a different city or a change in career. The default mode most of these relationships do is to go stagnant. Then you run into each other 5 years later and while there is rapport, you don't have the same connection you used to.

It's important to spend a little time maintaining special relationships you have with people, if only for the fact that it's sad to lose a good relationship with someone you got along with so well.

Because we're time poor, I advocate making an annual phone call to say hello and catch up what's going on in their lives. I usually do these at Christmas, but it could equally be done one their birthday, the end of the financial year, whatever. It's a small time investment to maintain a special relationship you had with someone and they will usually appreciate it.

I don't do this for every relationship, because I wouldn't have time. Just the special ones.

Example:

Anne was a financial controller looking to step up to a proper CFO role. It was difficult at her current firm as the current CFO had been in the firm 20 years and was only in his mid-forties, with no plans to change companies. She wasn't keen on making a sideways move with the hope of stepping up to a CFO role in the future.

Anne spoke with a long-term mentor of hers, Andrew (a Sales Director), who she met in a formal mentoring program 5 years ago; they still stay in touch. Anne had used her background as a financial controller and auditor to help Andrew identify a sales rep in his team who had been cheating the company with fraudulent expenses. It's fair to say that Anne saved Andrew's job by allowing him to proactively deal with the situation.

She outlined her career challenge with Andrew and he used his C-level contacts in his role as head of sales at his company to identify a firm who required a CFO with her background. He went in to bat for her, hard, putting his (and his company's) reputation on the line if she didn't work out.
He knew Anne would succeed, and that if she did, it would only improve the relationship with that customer.

Anne was hired, and flourished in the new role. Without Andrew's assistance she would have had a much tougher time landing the right position and would have risked moving into a role she wasn't suited to.

Because they trusted each other, once she was in the role, Anne and Andrew were able to have unusually open conversations about budget availability at her company, and came up with a way to fix a short-term budget issue with a creative solution which resulted in a $3 million dollar deal for Andrew's company. Both Anne and Andrew were recognised internally for what they *achieved at their respective companies, a by-product of one person helping another person they trusted enough to bet their reputation on.*

Chapter 6. Entering the Trust Matrix

Many industries are tight-knit. You need to "break into the industry". The good news is that once you're in, there is a high "barrier to entry" for your competition. Tight-knit industries tend to rely more heavily on the Trust Matrix, because they are closed to outsiders that don't know anybody. It's not what you know, it's who you know.

So how do you get your foot in the door when you don't know anyone? There are two key things you need to be doing regardless, but they apply doubly when you're trying to break into a new industry:

Take the initiative:

Nobody's going to walk up to you and say "Gee whiz, you're just standing here and seem to have some relevant qualifications. How'd you like to come and work for us?"

No way! You've got to put yourself out there however you can - that means reaching out to people you don't know, asking for introductions, and adding value however you can.

Add value:

Nobody's going to want anything to do with you if you aren't adding value. It doesn't matter what you're bringing to the table, but you need to understand how you're adding value to somebody and make sure you're consistently delivering on that value. If you're doing that, the opportunities will come.

For new graduates

If you're at the beginning of your career, you don't have a lot of career capital. You might have a qualification, but you don't have any experience or a professional network. What do you have to offer?

1. Low salary expectations
2. Energy
3. Attitude
4. An option on your future potential

Don't be choosy. Get your foot in the door of the industry of your choice and you can work your way up from there. Treat it like an apprenticeship, and focus on compounding your skills, knowledge and experience to position yourself favourably to seize future opportunities.

Apprenticeships have been around in one form or another for a very long time, and in the professional world, the concept is as valid as someone wanting to become a plumber.

Having a portfolio of work you've undertaken while studying or as personal projects is a great way to set yourself apart from the crowd, and hiring managers will be impressed. It demonstrates that you have a genuine interest in your chosen profession, and are able to put your qualifications into practice.

As a total greenhorn, you can work under a group of experienced co-workers, some of whom can act as mentors to help you master your craft. The key to getting a mentor (in the workplace this is best done informally) is to be the kind of person that more experienced people will want to mentor.

You need to be humble, willing to learn, have the right attitude, and show that you're hardworking and willing to put the advice into practice. There's nothing worse than seeing valuable advice be ignored by someone who really should be putting it to good use.

Once someone's mentored you, they'll be looking out for you and keen to help you succeed - and you'll have more supporters to carry your reputation through the Trust Matrix.

It's actually much easier to make a good first impression as a very young person because many young people don't understand the basics of things like showing up on time and paying attention to people when they're talking to them. By mastering the basics outlined in chapter 3 you're already one step ahead.

Small advantages at the early stages of your career will carry you through and compound throughout your career. Being the first to get promoted, getting access to interesting projects, and being mentored by key leaders in a business will give you additional advantages you can build on as you progress through the subsequent stages of your career.

Don't be afraid of failure - taking well-calculated career risks almost always pays off, and even if it doesn't you'll have valuable experience and more grit. The worst that will happen is you take a temporary step backwards before going forward again. Just make sure you have a mentor who can intervene if you decide to do something which will turn out to be monumentally stupid.

For experienced people

If you're transitioning from another industry where you have 10+ years of experience, you're bringing career capital you can leverage. There are right ways and wrong ways to use that career capital.

Tapping your extended network is a good starting point to identify people you can connect with in a new industry. You should be moving into an industry for the right reasons (for example, you're interested in the industry and have something to offer) not because your current industry reputation is in tatters or you've heard it's a good way to make a lot of money.

By using your network, you are effectively leveraging the Trust Matrix to move from one industry to another, using your connections and reputation to make the transition easier. Yes, you might need some kind of qualification, but without the right network to leverage your newly-acquired skills, you'll be stuck trying to get in through the front door and competing with all the graduates. Put that career capital to work!

Remember that when it comes to winning people over, attitude is everything. You're effectively starting again at the bottom, and it's healthy to approach your first opportunity in a humble manner. You'll likely find ways you can apply your existing knowledge and connections into the new role.

If you're transitioning into an industry which has suddenly become hot, be wary of the fact that industry veterans might see you as someone joining the bandwagon because it looks like an easy way to make money.

This won't be their opinion forever, but be conscious that some people will see you this way, and fortunately there are a couple of things you can do to ingratiate yourself into the industry:

1. Take things you've learned from your other industry and apply it to the industry you're in now. For example, if you were selling new cars and have transitioned to selling IT Managed Services, you can show sales teams how important it is to give the customer a great buying experience, and how to strategically position upsells to maximise the size of the deal.

2. Approach the industry with an attitude of humbleness and an eagerness to learn - there's no such thing as a stupid question. While people can't help judging a book by its cover initially, you'll be able to quickly overcome any prejudice by bringing the same energy a 22-year-old graduate would do when you're a 55-year-old who still has 10 years of runway to achieve great things before they are likely to retire.

Example:

Henry was a former professional athlete who retired from sports at the age of 34 and tried his hand at a few post-athletic careers with limited success. Now in his early forties, he got an entry-level sales position with a business automation product, at the time a hot part of the industry. The technology was pretty complicated, and Henry wasn't confident that he would be successful. The hiring manager, who had been a fan of Henry's during his athletic career, encouraged him.

"Henry, the way this product works is too complicated for any of our sales people. You've got a sales engineer to help you with the technology stuff, but what this product

really does is help teams work together more effectively. You know what it's like to work in a team, and what causes a team to either work smoothly or become disconnected. Let's work together on a few stories from your athletic career that you can use to sell the vision of the product."

After some practice and mentoring from his new boss, Henry started leveraging his strengths to get different divisions of his prospect companies to all agree on how the technology would transform the business. In his second year Henry was #1 sales representative in his region and went to president's club. At their next sales kickoff, he led his region again, and was invited on stage to speak about his journey and how he used his background and experience to sell a product that he still (proudly) admits he doesn't understand.

Networking Events

I don't make a habit of going to networking events myself but they are a great way to build your network in a new industry.

There is plenty of awkwardness at networking events, so don't worry about getting embarrassed. The purpose is to get comfortable talking to people and hopefully make a few contacts.

1. Approach people on their own and introduce yourself. People standing awkwardly on their own are dying for someone to talk to and you have just broken the ice by going up to them.
2. Don't interrupt groups of 2 who are facing one another - it might be a personal conversation. Those who have an open gap you can step into and introduce yourself will be more welcoming.
3. Don't treat it as a dating opportunity - it's not appropriate in professional settings and a great

way for your name to be attached to dickhead behaviour.

4. Don't talk about yourself - keep asking questions of the other person. When someone answers a question, ask another question based on their answer. If you keep asking them about themselves they'll think you're the most interesting person they've ever met. We have two ears and one mouth for a reason.

5. Relax and enjoy it. Don't worry about making errors, consider any networking event to simply be practice to prepare you for higher-stakes situations.

In the early stages of building your network, you want to go for volume - meet as many people as you can. This way you can start spreading your name around or at least become known to lots of people. Connect with them on LinkedIn so you've got a way to get in touch, but don't ask them for any favours just now - you just want to make the connection.

You might not know much, but if you connect with a more senior person in a different industry (for example, if you're in Cybersecurity, and they're a Financial Controller) you will suddenly become the most knowledgeable Cybersecurity person they know, and treat you like some sort of expert. Even though you're more junior, your knowledge and experience will add value to them.

Let's suppose this more senior person could use your help - maybe they have a role organising morning briefing sessions and want someone to conduct a session about Cybersecurity - suddenly you're invited to present and get the opportunity to build your brand with 30 other people. Boom, you're starting to scale your reach into the Trust Matrix for this particular industry. As a junior person, your Cybersecurity IQ might only be 95, but in a room full of accountants whose Cybersecurity IQ is 75, you'll be considered a genius. In fact, your knowledge is better suited to newbies, because it will be more accessible to them, especially if you focus on the few core principles that your industry operates on.

One of the most useful skills you will ever acquire is public speaking. Making the commitment to attend a Toastmasters club for at least 2 years in the early stages of your career will pay huge dividends throughout your life, both professionally and personally. I can't recommend it highly enough to increase your ability to add value, and make a great impression on a large group of people whenever you have the opportunity to deliver a speech.

Chapter 7. First Impressions Matter

People say you never get a second chance to make a first impression. That's true, and if people thought about this more, they'd make a lot more of an effort to show their best selves when they meet someone for the first time.

Make a bad first impression, and not only will you have an uphill battle to recover your reputation (a campaign that could take a year or longer) you could be shut out from any opportunity to even do this because they'll have already decided they want nothing to do with you.

Conversely, there are plenty of bad operators out there who coast through their careers off the back of their ability to make a great first impression, while their true colours aren't shown for months or even years.

First impressions are critical to forming relationships quickly that you can build on to become future trusted, long-term relationships. The good news is that this doesn't require a special strategy. It's purely about execution.

What is strategy vs execution? If strategy is all about your plan, execution is all about how well you do the steps. Many people in the business world over-emphasise strategy, when often it's much more important to execute well. If your strategy is to make a good first impression, and it should be, all you need to do is follow these basic rules consistently and be yourself.

Being yourself is important, because if you come across as inauthentic, this throws people off straight away. Don't try to be someone else - just be your confident, natural self while following the basic rules that make a good first impression.

Rules to making a good first impression

Nobody cares how smart you are if you don't get the basics right.

It's not complicated and doesn't require any special talent. But much like common sense, I'm amazed at how often people flout these rules, to their own detriment:

1. Show up early so you can always be on time.
2. Dress and groom yourself appropriately for the situation.
3. Stand straight and speak clearly.
4. Maintain a professional level of eye contact.
5. Listen more than you talk. You've got two ears and one mouth for a reason. Don't cut people off or interrupt them. Don't tell long stories about yourself.
6. Make professional conversation and avoid controversial topics.
7. Focus on the person you're speaking with and don't get distracted.
8. Remember the 5 P's: Prior Preparation Prevents Poor Performance. Lack of preparation is obvious and shows disrespect for the people who are giving their time to you.

9. If you commit to doing something, do it right
   away to show you're organised and on the ball.

Blind Spots

An exercise I'd recommend is to aggressively audit your
blind spots for idiosyncrasies that put people off when
their first meet you. Some people don't take well to
feedback, but we all have blind spots, and becoming
more self-aware is the first step to addressing them.

There's a good chance there is an aspect of your
personality that is really bothersome, and nobody is
willing to say it to your face (or they once tried and you
immediately got defensive).

Find one or more long-term friends that still interact with
you regularly and ask them to tell you the thing which is
most off-putting about you. Nobody will give you this
feedback unprompted or if they don't know you really
well. This is why you need to actively seek out feedback

with people who know and trust you. Instruct them to be brutally honest.

You should incorporate this with regular feedback from people who have just started interacting with you - regular feedback helps you improve in every aspect of life, but it's almost never given unprompted. You need to ask for it, listen to the feedback, and thank the person who is offering it. Many people get nervous about giving other people feedback so you need to make them feel comfortable with telling you the ugly truth.

I'm not referring to the harmless eccentricities that show a bit of personality and make you more memorable.

I'm talking about that major blind spots in your own manner which can seriously hold you back. It pays to aggressively seek them out and do your best to overcome them. Examples could include sounding overly pompous, swearing too much, or not giving others room to speak.

These things are all really noticeable, but people are unlikely to tell you about them unprompted. What these blind spots will do is leave a bad impression, and the people you're offending will hesitate before making the effort to bring you an opportunity, like a job recommendation, or a sale you could make with their company. You need to be operating well above the bare minimum to warrant someone putting their reputation on the line to bring you something of value.

The good news is that once the basic stuff is a habit, it's effortless to make a first impression nearly every time. A good first impression with everyone you meet is the foundation for an excellent reputation in the trust matrix.

Chapter 8. Quid Pro Quo

Quid pro quo is a Latin term meaning "something for something". It's natural that you'll want to leverage your network to help you achieve things, but life is a two-way street - remember the rule to give freely before asking others for favours.

When you want somebody to do something for you, it can either set you up for success and improved reputation; or failure and being known as a taker rather than a maker. What are makers and takers, you ask?

Makers create value and leave things better than they found them, takers smash and grab without giving freely in return. If you're a maker, you're constantly looking for ways to add value and make "deposits" into the Trust Matrix. If you're a taker, people will find out very quickly, and soon you'll have exhausted your "overdraft".

The golden rule is to give before you have received. Doing favours to help people is, again, like making deposits into a bank account that you hope to occasionally draw down on later. It shouldn't be your primary means of getting what you want, but it's a useful tool in the arsenal of a hardworking person with a good reputation.

Doing introductions

Favours frequently come in the form of an introduction to connect one person to another.

I like doing introductions for people because it means I'm helping two people out at once with very little effort on my part - I'm simply leveraging my existing network and reputation to create value out of thin air. Doing this also puts credits in the Trust Matrix bank that improves both people's opinion of me and means they're likely to return the favour in future.

To qualify for an introduction generally means the following:

1.   Both parties will benefit from the introduction.

2. I know you're a reliable person who will conduct themselves with integrity.

3. The person who I'm introducing you to is also a reliable person who will conduct themselves with integrity.

4. If I don't know you well but think it might still be a fit, I'll caveat an introduction with the following "I haven't worked with them and don't know them well, but based on the background might be a fit - over to you both".

5. I'll check with the other person for permission before making an introduction (blind introductions aren't polite, especially to busy people).

6. If you get an opportunity to do a favour for me in the future, I expect you to help me out if it's something small. I'm pretty good at telling who the takers are now, and when they ask me for things, I don't happen to be able to help.

It might seem harsh and self-serving not to help certain people but you can't encourage taker behaviour. This is the "give to get" economy at work. If you conduct yourself appropriately, people will help you out, and if you don't, you'll spend the rest of your life wondering why nobody is ever able to help you.

Guidelines for helping people

Be very cautious about helping people you don't know well. If someone you've just met is asking you for a recommendation, you should be wondering why they aren't asking someone who knows them better. Maybe the people who do know them better wouldn't recommend them.

Being known as the sort of person who can help with these introductions is great for your personal brand and creates more quid pro quo situations, so it's always good to at least look into whether you can help them. "Let me see if I know anybody" is all you need to say.

If someone comes to mind straight away I won't name them on the spot because that creates an expectation. First, I'll check with them to see if they're happy being introduced. After that, your job is done. An example introductory email here:

Dear Greg,

I had a think about who would be a fit for the sales role you're currently trying to fill - and I'm connecting you with Susan who I worked with 3 years ago at XYZ Telecoms.

She'd be open to having a chat about the role, so over to you both to see if there's a mutual fit.

That's all it takes - no expectations and no specific recommendations (unless you know someone well enough to strongly recommend them for certain skills that you're prepared to be on the hook for if they don't measure up).

I tend not to follow up on how it goes, but it's always satisfying to later find out that you've been able to help two people do a deal together.

What's the ask?

When requesting a favour from somebody else, it's good to be clear about what the "ask" is. There's no need to beat around the bush - be clear about what you would like that person to help you with. Some good general guidelines:

1. You should be in good enough standing with this person, and know them well enough, that you feel comfortable asking them to help you.

2. The favour you're asking should require a small amount of effort from your colleague but will be very helpful to you.

3. It should be easy for the person to say no. They're under no obligation to help you and making them feel pressured to do you a favour is just going to make them less willing to take your call in future.

4. Show your appreciation by whichever way is most appropriate. You be the judge.

Chapter 9. Keeping Secrets

We all have information that would be valuable (or cause damage) if it were to fall into the wrong hands. Protecting that information is a big responsibility and failure to do so could severely impact your reputation.

Just because you tell the truth, doesn't mean you should allow yourself to feel pressured to reveal information you shouldn't. In fact, sharing information you shouldn't be sharing shows the person who wants that information that you can't be trusted to keep a secret.

In these situations, it's also best to avoid knowingly misleading people just to throw them off the track. For example, if a salesperson you're dealing with asks you what your budget is for a project you're procuring a system for, you don't need to intentionally low-ball it just to throw them off the mark. Eventually, they'll find out what your budget is and you'll get a reputation for playing games with people. You're perfectly entitled to tell them "I can't share that information with you right now."

Sharing privileged information has its time and place. If you want to show someone that you trust them, you can share information, but you also risk the fact that they could go on to share this information with other parties. If you trust each other, you can be more willing to take the risk if it's to advance a common interest - a course of action commonly referred to as "opening the kimono".

Take the situation with a buyer for example. He needs to buy 300 new licenses of a software platform for a team they are integrating. Budgets are tight and they've historically paid $1000 per year for a license. They only have $250k in additional opex this year with which to make the purchase.

If the buyer trusts their vendor, they can say "Look - we're trying to minimise the expense here through to the end of the fiscal year. My budget is $250k, and I need 300 licenses. What can we do to work out a deal?"

Discounting to $833 per license is unlikely to get approved commercially and it's not a fair give-and-take negotiation.

What he might look into doing is financing the over budget component of the cost so that the expense can be deferred into the subsequent financial year. This solves the buyer's problem, builds further trust, and the seller has done the right thing by their company to achieve a fair commercial outcome that everyone is happy with.

Johnny Tight-lips

When in doubt, it's always good to err on the side of not sharing information, especially with people you don't know well. There are people who build their careers on taking advantage of the information they've gleaned from others, and using it to work angles themselves.

These people can actually be useful because they also tend to be blabbermouths. Be sure to get the information you can use to your advantage, but do not tell them anything you shouldn't - for obvious reasons.

Having a reputation for being a "vault" in gossip-heavy industries is like gold. People will trust you with confidential information and you'll be able to use it to better navigate the political landscape.

Get a reputation for loose lips, and you'll be kept in the dark because nobody trusts you.

Managing the minefield

Some situations can be highly sensitive, and you need to share some information but also run the risk of sharing too much. With experience, often comes wisdom, and while you're still early in your wisdom acquisition, you need to err on the side of caution to avoid doing the wrong thing.

Don't let people pressure you to share information you shouldn't. The easiest way to deflect these requests is ask them to imagine the shoe is on the other foot.

"Leon, why can't you tell me who you're working with on this deal?"

"Nigel, I'm sure you wouldn't want me going around blabbing about the deals we're working on together to my other partners. Let's focus on the opportunities we can work together on."

You will make mistakes from time to time, and some people will betray your trust. You can either complain about it, or consider it a useful lesson for the future.

Try to learn something from every situation like this - your experience will compound rapidly and equip you to handle very sensitive situations.

Chapter 10. Succeeding in a world of dickheads

It's sometimes the case that you find yourself in a situation where you're surrounded by dickheads. The Trust Matrix has collapsed in on itself to become a black hole of dodgy people where nothing gets done without something funny going on.

This is a convenient excuse for people who are looking for a reason to act like dickheads. The reality is, no matter what industry you are in, you alone make the choice about whether to rise above the corruption, leave that particular industry, or let the crabs drag you into the bucket with them:

The Crabs in a bucket analogy: If you put a large group of crabs into a bucket, and one tries to escape, the others pull it back in. Known in Australia as the "tall poppy syndrome". If the group sees you acting in a way that makes them feel inferior, they will seek to drag you down to their level.

If you find yourself in this situation, you've got 3 choices: Rise above, Quit the game altogether, or Join in with the crabs.

Rise above the corruption

Prepare to be disappointed at every turn by people who let you down. Do you know what the key to happiness is? Low expectations!

If you find yourself in a Trust Matrix where nobody trusts each other, then you need to operate on a mindset of "don't trust other people until they show signs that they can be trusted." If you open with this kind of approach, at the very least you'll position yourself as someone who isn't going to be bullshitted. You can work your way up from there with each person who demonstrates over time that they can conduct themselves with integrity.

Jim Rohn's excellent audiotape series "Cultivating an unshakeable character" refers to a business owner in the construction industry which was full of dickheads. His modus operandi was "You play straight with me, and I'll play straight with you".

Even amongst the dickheads, you'll find others like you who want to rise above it all. Team up with them by forming your own cluster of high-integrity people, and start working more closely together. Others will notice.

Leaving the industry

Don't let a few bad apples let you quit an industry, especially if you're doing well. The grass always appears to be greener on the other side, but the reality is that the grass is greenest on the side of the fence that you water the most.

Many people choose to concentrate on everything that's wrong with their current situation, instead of gratitude for what's good, and taking action on the things over which they have control.

You can't stop someone from deciding to screw you over, but you can decide how you'll respond, and what you can reasonably do to not let it happen again.

If you decide you really do want to leave an industry, that's when it's good to be plugged into other clusters of people that you can lean on to help you make a smooth transition into a better situation. No matter what your current situation is, doing the right thing always pays off in the long run.

Letting the crabs drag you into the bucket

You're not seriously considering this option are you? Haven't you been paying attention?

The Trust Matrix doesn't just exist to reward the right behaviour. It also punishes people who take this course of action, and as someone now enlightened to how the Trust Matrix works, I'm sure you won't let a few dickheads spoil your own personal integrity.

Admittedly, it's very tempting to go with the flow since "everybody else is doing it".

If you do that, you've recognised a problem; and instead of contributing to its resolution, you've decided to help make the problem worse. That is a choice you will have made of your own free will, and you'll need to live with the consequences of your decision.

I know a dickhead, can I fix them?

No.

Some people are born dickheads, and some people become dickheads over time. Either way, it's not your job to fix them, and you are asking for trouble if you try.

From Matthew 7:6 in Jesus' sermon on the mount:

"Do not give what is holy to the dogs; nor cast your pearls before swine, lest they trample them under their feet, and turn and tear you into pieces."

Trying to help a dickhead is a fool's errand for the following reasons:

1. If they are unaware, that's because they don't listen to feedback. I guarantee you someone has tried to help them in the past and has decided never to attempt such a thing again after observing their reaction.
2. If they are aware, then they enjoy being a dickhead. Don't be the one to spoil their fun because they clearly enjoy it.
3. Your time and energy are better spent on more productive activities.

You'll definitely want to avoid inadvertently ending up with a dickhead as a boss. Here are some good questions to ask during the interview process:

1. Tell me about your leadership style? (Be wary of corporate BS-speak or obvious signs of poor leadership like micromanagement or overly aggressive style)

2. What's been your proudest personal achievement in this role so far? (The answer should be all about their team and not all about them)
3. What's an example of something new you've learned about leadership in the last 12 months (A leader who thinks there is nothing else to learn is either already a dickhead or on their way to becoming one)

Chapter 11. When someone badmouths you

It's a fact of life that eventually, someone somewhere is going to put your name into disrepute. You can't please everyone all the time, and even if you conduct yourself with total integrity at every interaction (something for us all to strive for even if it's unlikely to ever be achievable); sooner or later, somebody is going to go around telling everyone they know that you're a dickhead.

This is where a strong positive reputation in the Trust Matrix really helps. You'll have an army of people who will either defend you without you present, or at the very least, take your criticism with a grain of salt.

The best way to protect your reputation is to have a good one already that other people can't easily damage.

Take this quote from Robert Greene's 48 Laws of Power, Chapter 5: So much depends on reputation, guard it with your life:

"A solid reputation increases your presence and exaggerates your strengths without you having to spend much energy. It can also create an aura around you that will instil respect, even fear. Your reputation inevitably precedes you, and if it inspires respect, a lot of your work is done for you before you arrive on the scene or utter a single word."

Dickheads will rarely badmouth you to your face. They'll drop hints to others, or loudly sully your reputation around people who know them and trust them, further spreading the damage. Getting into defence mode can be seen as a sign of weakness or an admission of guilt. In my experience, the best response is to scoff and correct the record to the people you heard it from. If you have a good reputation already, people are much more likely to believe you.

Be sure to also address the badmouthing in a professional manner to its originator. They'll most likely deny it, or justify it with an exaggerated story, but it's important to show you don't take any crap from people. They'll quickly learn that you don't accept being spoken about in this manner, and that you are surrounded by plenty of people who think highly of you.

Correct them on their error, let them make whatever denials or convenient explanations they see fit to make, and in the future, watch them like a hawk.

Gossip is unavoidable

It's human nature that we are going to gossip about other people behind their backs, and before you know it the stories have spread multiple degrees of separation away from the source, and in a vastly exaggerated form.

It's also human nature that the bad stories are going to travel much further than the stories about what someone did well - even if what they did was pretty extraordinary.

Because these things are outside your control, and would be a waste of time and energy to try and police, you need to fight negative messaging about you using the old "high road" method, which I'm sure you can guess if you've gotten this far:

If you do the right thing all the time, it's less likely that people will say bad things about you!

You can't avoid it 100%, nor should you waste energy trying to. What you can do is have a long and well-known track record of being a reliable and trustworthy person.

Your track record is a key asset to anchor your position in the Trust Matrix and have it be resilient to pot-shots from critics who insist on spreading their own half-baked opinions.

Don't believe everything you hear

There's a lesson here for people on the receiving end of gossip as well - take anything negative you hear with a grain of salt. Juicy gossip has an addictive quality to it and people love sharing stories, without verifying them for truth.

It is also, however, an unfortunate reality that there's no smoke without fire. Not only is it going to be hard to give someone the benefit of the doubt based on the gossip, it would be naive to ignore the stories - especially if they all paint a consistent picture.

Chapter 12. How to fix a bad reputation

If you've gotten this far and have concluded that you are, in fact, a dickhead, I congratulate you for possessing a level of self-awareness that already makes you less of a dickhead.

I'm glad this book has been a wake-up call to you. I haven't actually been in this situation myself (although I'm sure there are people out there who think I'm a dickhead) so my guidance below is only based on what conduct I'd like to see from someone I already regard as a dickhead.

Recognise also that some people are never going to deal with you, no matter what you do. Your reputation is a result of past behaviour, something which is now totally outside your control. You could have conducted yourself differently in the past, but that ship has sailed. It's time to make a real change and look to a better future.

What makes a bad reputation?

Bad reputations can come as a result of one or more of the following characteristics:

A poor performer or "C-Player":

If you're a mediocre performer, focus on first meeting the standards of your current role, then excelling so you can be justified in moving up. Your past does not dictate your future, and the best way to get to A-player status is to display a positive attitude, take feedback from others, and learn from your mistakes.

Focus on meeting the KPI's set by your manager and actively ask for feedback on how to improve. Most leaders don't want to have the difficult conversations to address poor performance and are relieved more than anything when the problem fixes itself.

A flaky person who doesn't meet commitments:

While not a dealbreaker in itself, this attribute will make it difficult to access new opportunities if you're known as someone who either won't take on the job, or generates lots of excuses. Flaky people also tend to be really good at first impressions and sweeping their shortcomings under the rug with a cheery demeanour and dismissive excuses.

The solution is to acknowledge when you let someone down and promise to do better in the future. Focus on small wins and try to always deliver what you commit to people. It's ok to say no, if you know you won't be able to do something.

Being arrogant:

This is the kind of behaviour that acts as a gateway to full-on dickhead territory in future, and people are unlikely to directly call you on it - you'll just be referred to as arrogant behind your back and people will prefer not to deal with you. After you've left a company, newer people who have never met you will hear the stories about what an arrogant jerk you were.

The best solution to discover whether you display traits of arrogance (Especially if you think you're special and the occasional arrogance is justified); ask people close to you to honestly tell you if you're arrogant, and if so, have them provide examples.

Problems with drugs/alcohol or any other addiction:

If you can't handle it in moderation you need to go clean. It's also a problem that is hard for your boss to address because allegations of an addiction are a HR minefield. You need to be seriously dropping the ball for it to be taken up - so you need to address it yourself.

This is actually a fairly simple fix because if you go clean and suddenly change the way you work with people they will assume the addictions were the problem and give you a clean slate to get back on track. Don't be afraid to ask for help and find a new mix of friends that make it harder for you to fall off the wagon.

Lacking Integrity:

This will never totally go away - once bitten, twice shy. You will need to rebuild your integrity one interaction at a time, and acknowledge to people you have mistreated in the past that you're now trying to live life differently. Don't expect them to believe you - your actions will do all the talking, and it will take time to win back any level of trust with them.

Being a taker, not a maker:

People who ask inappropriate favours lose friends extremely quickly. Stop asking people for favours all the time without contributing value yourself. Most people will be too polite to call you on this, so it's up to you to recognise it.

If you have a track record of being a taker, look at the people you took favours from and try to find a way to redress the balance. They will appreciate it, having written you off as a taker already. Like the flaky individual, this requires a 180-degree habit change.

Chapter 13. Application

I hope this book has opened your eyes to how the Trust Matrix works, and given you concrete steps you can take to build a positive personal brand which radiates beyond your immediate network into the Trust Matrix.

You should be able to notice how your behaviour impacts the relationships around you and how it affects your reputation over time. When in doubt, refer back to the rules as a set of core principles on how to operate effectively within the Trust Matrix.

Even though we're all treading our own paths, we needn't run the race alone. The people closest to you are going to act as superconductors, spreading the message of your positive attributes out to their extended networks.

This book will likely prompt you to first look externally at whom you do and do not trust.

Instead, I encourage you to first hold the mirror up to yourself. Are you a person that others can confidently rely upon to conduct themselves with integrity?

If everyone in the business world did this, it would be impossible for dickheads to build their careers without first undergoing a serious attitude adjustment.

Whether or not you've heard about it, the Trust Matrix is real.

The more of us that are conscious of its power, the better.

Further Reading

Dale Carnegie: How to Win Friends and Influence People

This book is first, because it's the gold standard of building relationships. The title sounds vaguely manipulative, but if I distilled the entire book into a sentence, it's to have a genuine interest in everybody you meet.

Reid Hoffman - Startup of you

The section on networking is great additional reading to this book and echoes a lot of the points I make around how to meet new people.

Robert Greene - 48 Laws of Power

Whether you want to play or not, you can't deny the power game exists. This book is a classic and outlines what you need to be aware of so you don't get blindsided by office politics. Is there was one law to commit to heart, let it be law 5: So much depends on your reputation, guard it with your life.

Naval Ravikant - How to get rich (Without getting lucky)

This isn't a book but a series of tweets Naval put out in 2018 - A lot of his principles apply only to those who put the Trust Matrix to work for them. Just Google "Naval Twitter Storm".

Jim Rohn - Cultivating an unshakable character

This is an audio program, and the defining work on how to become a true person of integrity and reliability.

Want to keep in touch?

Let me know if this book worked for you by emailing me at trustmatrixbook@gmail.com

www.ingramcontent.com/pod-product-compliance
Lightning Source LLC
Chambersburg PA
CBHW030529210326
41597CB00013B/1085